Standing Firm in These Last Days

KAY ARTHUR

HARVEST HOUSE™ PUBLISHERS

EUGENE, OREGON

The New Inductive Study Series
STANDING FIRM IN THESE LAST DAYS

Copyright © 1996 by Precept Ministries International
Published by Harvest House Publishers
Eugene, Oregon 97402

Library of Congress Cataloging-in-Publication Data
Arthur, Kay, 1933–
    Standing firm in these last days / Kay Arthur.
      p. cm. — (The new inductive study series)
    Includes bibliographical references.
    ISBN 0-7369-0812-9 (alk. paper)
    1. Bible. N.T. Thessalonians—Study and teaching. I. Title. II. Series: Arthur, Kay, 1933–
    The new inductive study series.
BS2725.5.A78 1996
227'.8'007—dc20   96-34329
                                                                 CIP

02 03 04 05 06 07 08 09 10 / BP-MS / 10 9 8 7 6 5 4 3 2 1

Contents

How to Get Started...

WHEN ALL ELSE FAILS, READ THE DIRECTIONS!

Let's face it, most of us think that directions are meant to be read only if we can't figure out what to do on our own. Reading directions slows us down and keeps us from getting on with the matter at hand. I understand. I feel the very same way! However, the brief directions which follow are an integral part of your study and will save you time and frustration in the long run, so take a few minutes and begin well!

FIRST

Let's talk about what you are going to need in order to do this study. In addition to this book, you will need three "tools":

1. A Bible. (*The New Inductive Study Bible [NISB]* is *the* ideal Bible for this type of study because of the single-column text, easy-to-read type, high-quality paper, wide margins, and innumerable study helps.) However, no matter which Bible you choose for this study, be aware that you will be instructed to mark its pages. So if you prefer not to mark in your Bible and you have access to a Bible program and a computer, you could print out the text of 1 and 2 Thessalonians and work from your printout. Or you could photocopy the text of 1 and 2 Thessalonians from

your Bible and work on that copy. (This is only permissible *if* it is for your own use.)

2. A four-color ballpoint pen, various colored fine-point pens, colored pencils, or an eight-color Pentel pencil (available from Precept Ministries International or at most office supply stores).

3. A composition book or notebook for working on your assignments and recording your insights and/or observations. Record your insights chapter by chapter, noting new chapter headings (chapter 1, chapter 2, and so on) as you move through the study.

SECOND

If you are doing this study within the framework of a group and find that you are not able to do each day's study in any given week, simply do what you can. Doing a little is better than doing nothing. Don't be an all-or-nothing person when it comes to Bible study.

Remember that when you get into God's Word, you enter into intensive warfare with the devil (our enemy). In Ephesians 6 we see that every piece of the Christian's spiritual armor relates to the Word of God. Our main offensive weapon is the sword of the Spirit, which Ephesians tells us is the Word of God. Satan wants you to fight with a dull sword. Don't cooperate! You don't have to! Just recognize that it's warfare.

As you study 1 and 2 Thessalonians, you will be given specific instructions for each day. Each assignment will take about 15 to 30 minutes, depending on what is covered that day. Although you will have these specific daily instructions, there are basic things you need to know, do, and remember as you move through the books chapter by chapter. So let's cover these together now.

1. As you read each chapter, train yourself to ask the "5 W's and an H": who, what, when, where, why, and how. Asking questions like these helps you see exactly what the Word of God is saying. When you interrogate the text with the 5 W's and an H, you'll ask questions like this:

    a. **What** is the chapter about?
    b. **Who** are the main characters?
    c. **When** does this event or teaching take place?
    d. **Where** does this happen?
    e. **Why** is this being done or said?
    f. **How** did it happen?

2. The time references indicating the "when" of events and teachings are very important and should be marked in an easily recognizable way in your Bible. We suggest putting a clock (like the one shown here) in the margin of your Bible beside the verse where the time phrase occurs. You may prefer to draw the clock over the time-related word or phrase, or you may simply want to underline or color the references to time in one specific color.

Remember, time and chronological sequence may be expressed in a number of ways: by mentioning a specific time, day, month, or year or by mentioning a specific event that clues you in to the time, such as a feast, a year of a king's reign, etc. Time may also be noted by words such as *then, when, afterwards, at this time*, etc.

3. There are key words you will want to color-code in the text of your Bible throughout your study. This is the reason for your colored pencils or pens. Developing the habit of marking your Bible in this way will make a significant difference in the effectiveness of your study and how much you remember.

A **key word** is an important word used by the author repeatedly to convey his message to the reader. In the same way that a key unlocks a door, key words unlock the meaning of the text. Certain key words or phrases will show up throughout the book as a whole, while others will be concentrated in specific chapters or segments of the book. When you color-code a key word, be sure to mark its synonyms in the same way you mark the key word. (Remember that a synonym is a word that has the same meaning in the context as the key word you are marking.) Also mark pronouns that refer to the key word in the same way you are marking the word (*he, his, she, her, it, we, they, us, our, you, them, their*).

Marking key words allows you to identify the word and, thus, the sense of the text easily. You can mark words using colors, symbols, or a combination of both. However, colors are easier to distinguish than symbols when looking back at the text of your Bible. If you use symbols, try to keep them very simple. For example, I use a megaphone to mark the word *gospel* and then color it green: gospel. I mark the words **suffering** and **affliction** using a red pen and a symbol that looks like flames. I mark every reference to the coming of the Lord Jesus Christ in a cloud like this:

the coming of the Lord Jesus Christ.

After the cloud is drawn, I color the outside margins of the cloud blue and fill in the center with yellow.

Color draws your eye quickly to the word and trains it to recognize the word. A symbol conveys the meaning of the word. It may seem a little juvenile to mark words in this way, but if you will get past that feeling and cultivate the habit of marking key words in your Bible in a distinctive and memorable way, you will see a significant difference in your ability to retain what you study.

Let me give you another example of how to mark words. You can mark references to any of the Godhead with yellow to show the unity between the three, and then in order to distinguish between the Father, Son, and Holy Spirit, you can draw a distinct symbol for each of the three with a purple pen. Mark the Father with a triangle like this: God symbolizing the Trinity. Mark the Son with the same triangle incorporating a cross in this way: Jesus , and mark the Holy Spirit with the triangle incorporating a cloud like this: Spirit .

You should devise a color-coding system for marking key words throughout your Bible so that when you look at the pages later, your eye will be drawn to the key words that you've marked. Once you begin color-coding key words, it's easy to forget what symbols or colors you are using to identify a particular word. You may wish to use the bottom portion of the perforated card in the back of this book to write the key words on. Mark the words the way you plan to mark them in your Bible and then use the card as a bookmark. You may want to make one bookmark for words marked consistently throughout your Bible and a different one for each specific book as you study.

In this study course, when you are instructed to mark a key word or phrase, you are given the New American Standard translation of the word or phrase. However, since other translations may translate a particular word or phrase from the Hebrew or Greek into English differently than the NASB, the King James Version (KJV), the New King James Version (NKJV), and the New International Version (NIV) equivalents are noted in a footnote and listed in the back of this book.

4. Since locations are very important when studying a historical or biographical book of the Bible, you will also want to mark these in a distinguishable way. We suggest simply double-underlining every reference to a location in green (grass and trees are green!). You won't find many locations to mark in Thessalonians. But when you do see a location mentioned, marking it will give you a greater appreciation of what is being said.

It is also helpful to look up locations on maps to get a proper perspective of where things are occurring in relationship to each other. Using maps in this way will give you the "geographical" context. If you have a *New Inductive Study Bible (NISB)*, you will find maps pertinent to a particular passage placed right in the text for ready reference. The maps are included in the Bible text so that you can tell where in the world it happened!

5. Every day when you finish your lesson, meditate on what you saw and ask your heavenly Father how you should live considering the truths you have just seen. At times, depending on how God has spoken to you, you might even want to record these "Lessons for Life" (LFL) in the margin of your Bible by the verses that contain the truth you are applying to your life. Put "LFL" in the margin of your Bible and then as briefly as possible record the lesson for life you want to remember under this heading.

6. Always begin your study with prayer. As you do your part to handle the Word of God accurately, remember that the Bible is a divinely inspired book. The words you are reading are truth, given to you by God that you might know Him and His ways. These truths are divinely revealed.

> For to us God revealed them through the Spirit;
> for the Spirit searches all things, even the depths
> of God. For who among men knows the thoughts
> of a man except the spirit of the man which is in
> him? Even so the thoughts of God no one knows
> except the Spirit of God (1 Corinthians 2:10,11).

Therefore, ask God to reveal His truth to you, to lead you and guide you into all truth. He will, if you will ask.

THIRD

This study is designed to encourage you to spend time in the Word of God on a *daily* basis. Since man does not live by bread alone but by every word that comes out of the mouth of God, we each need a daily helping of truth.

The weekly assignments cover all seven days; however, the seventh day is different from the other days. On the seventh day, the focus is on one or more major truths covered in that week's study. You will find a verse or two to memorize and STORE IN YOUR HEART. Then there is a passage to READ AND DISCUSS. This section will be extremely profitable for those who are using this material in a class setting because it will cause the class to focus their attention on a critical portion of Scripture. To aid the individual and/or the class, there's a set of QUESTIONS FOR DISCUSSION OR INDIVIDUAL STUDY. This section is followed with a THOUGHT FOR THE WEEK which will help you understand how to walk in the light of what you've learned.

When you discuss each week's lesson, be sure the answers and insights are supported from the Bible itself rather than opinion or just consensus. Using the Scripture in its context to support your answers develops the habit of "handling the Word accurately." Always examine your insights by carefully observing the text to see what it *says*. Then before you decide the *meaning* of a Scripture or a passage, make sure you interpret it in the light of its context.

Scripture will never contradict Scripture. If it ever seems to be contradictory, you can be assured that somewhere something is being taken out of its context. Therefore, when you come to a passage that is difficult to deal with, reserve your interpretations for a time when you can study the passage in greater depth.

Books in The New Inductive Study Series are survey courses. If you wish to do more in-depth study of a particular book of the Bible, we would suggest using the Precept Upon Precept Bible study course on that book. More information on Precept Upon Precept Bible studies and where they are being taught can be obtained by contacting Precept Ministries International at 800-763-8280, visiting our website at www.precept.org, or filling out and mailing the response card in the back of this book.

Now then, reading the directions wasn't too bad, was it? You are on your way. Remember the prize is never given to those who don't finish the course...so "hangeth thou in there!"

FIRST THESSALONIANS

INTRODUCTION TO
1 THESSALONIANS

∾∾∾∾

Jesus is coming…and I'm filled with questions: *How should I live in the light of His coming? How am I going to handle the pressures of society? The cravings of my flesh?*

Should I stop working and do nothing but "serve Him" until He comes? Or should I grab all I can from life in case Jesus comes before I have tasted all that life has to offer?

What about the suffering and affliction I've encountered since I came to believe in Jesus Christ? Are those who scorned, mocked, and even afflicted me going to get away with their cruel and unfeeling behavior? Is there justice—a day of reckoning, or will His coming preclude all that?

What will His coming be like? What will happen to those who hoped to see His coming but died before He came? What will happen to those who believe and are here when He comes? If the day of the Lord is coming and it's a day of darkness and destruction, where will I be when it comes?

Beloved, if these are questions that cross your mind from time to time or maybe even linger there, then you have chosen just the right book to study. As you study these next nine weeks, you will find not only answers to these questions, but you will find valuable words of exhortation and comfort to equip you to stand firm and be found "without blame at the coming of our Lord Jesus Christ" (1 Thessalonians 5:23).

If you will give this study approximately 15 to 30 minutes each day, you will be awed at what you learn and at the transformation that results as you simply put the truths you glean into action. Studying the Word of God in this manner is transforming because you are brought face-to-face with the Word of God in a way that allows you to see truth for yourself. Remember that truth sets you apart unto your God and Father.

WITHOUT BLAME AT CHRIST'S RETURN—IS IT POSSIBLE?

ᑫᑫᑫᑫ

DAY ONE

Whenever you begin a study of any book of the Bible, if possible it is always good to read through the entire book several times to develop a sense of the context, an awareness of the total content of the book, and how the author lays out the material. However, due to the abbreviated nature of this series, you will be asked to read 1 Thessalonians as a whole only twice in this first week of our study.

Then next week, our five-week chapter-by-chapter analysis of 1 Thessalonians begins. Hopefully, after this six-week study, you will move on into the three-week study of 2 Thessalonians. As mentioned earlier, it is in the study of these two books that you will find the answers to the questions posed in the introduction to this study.

As you begin today, remember that marking key words in your Bible is an invaluable learning tool. (If you haven't read "How to Get Started" in the beginning of this book, please stop and do so now. It is critical to your study.) If you are hesitant to mark in your Bible because you think you may make mistakes, either print out a copy of the text from your computer or photocopy the text from your Bible so that you can work on a copy and transfer your marks and notations into your Bible later. In this age of erasers and correction fluid, don't be too reluctant to mark your Bible.

Now then, let's begin. Remember that our goal for this week is simply to get an overview of 1 Thessalonians. Don't become overwhelmed or bogged down by trying to understand the entire book in one reading.

1. Before you begin to read, make a bookmark listing the key words and phrases which follow. Mark them on the bookmark the same way you plan to mark them in the text:

- all references to the Lord's coming,

- *affliction*[1] and its synonyms—*afflictions*,[2] *tribulation, suffer(ed)*, and *suffering(s)*[3].

(Note that a specific phrase for the Lord's coming was not given since these references vary in their wording. You should decide how you will mark such references and mark the phrase "the Lord's coming" in this way on your bookmark and then watch carefully for and mark each reference in this way as you study.)

2. Read chapter 1 and then record the following in your notebook:

- Who is writing?

- To whom is it written?

3. Now on a different sheet of paper from the one where you just made your notes, make a list like the one on page 19, leaving space after each entry so that you have room to make notes related to each chapter as you study:

MAIN TOPICS IN 1 THESSALONIANS
    Chapter 1:
    Chapter 2:
    Chapter 3:
    Chapter 4:
    Chapter 5:

4. Now under your heading "Chapter 1," record the main subject or topic the author covers in this chapter. (By the way, there were no chapter divisions in the original text of the Bible. Chapter and verse divisions were added later for the sake of reference and study.)

DAY TWO

Read 1 Thessalonians 2 and continue to mark key words. Mark any reference to *the coming of Jesus Christ* and references to affliction by marking *suffered, sufferings,* or *mistreated*.[4] Be sure to mark key words with the color or symbol you chose when you made your bookmark yesterday.

Record the main subject the author covers in this chapter in your notebook under your Chapter 2 heading.

DAY THREE

Your assignment for today is to read chapter 3 and mark all references to *the coming of Jesus Christ* and any occurrence of the word *afflictions*[5] along with its synonyms. Don't forget to make your notes on the chapter in your notebook.

DAY FOUR

As you have probably already surmised, chapter 4 is your assignment for today. Follow the same procedure as for the previous chapters.

DAY FIVE

Finally, we come to the last chapter of 1 Thessalonians. Follow the same procedure you have in the last four days.

If you have time when you finish your assignment, look at your notebook to see what you recorded as the main subjects in each chapter. See if you notice where there seems to be a change or "break" in what the author is saying, a place where the book appears to take a different direction. If you see it, note it on your paper. It will be a topic for discussion on Day 7.

DAY SIX

Now that you have read 1 Thessalonians chapter by chapter, read straight through the entire book in one sitting. Again, watch for a natural division in the book. You may have seen this break yesterday when you reviewed your notes, but if you didn't see it try to notice it now. Watch carefully what Paul covers in the first three chapters, and then notice how chapter 4 opens. What shift does Paul's letter make in its contents and/or direction?

DAY SEVEN

Store in your heart: 1 Thessalonians 5:23.

Read and discuss: If you are studying in a group setting, choose four people to read the last three verses of each of the first four chapters of 1 Thessalonians. Then have a fifth person read 1 Thessalonians 5:23-28.

If you are studying on your own, simply read these verses for yourself.

QUESTIONS FOR DISCUSSION OR INDIVIDUAL STUDY

∾ According to the text, who is the author of 1 Thessalonians?

∾ To whom was 1 Thessalonians written?

∾ According to 1 Thessalonians 5:27, what *kind* of literature or writing is 1 Thessalonians?

∾ Where did the words *affliction(s)* or its synonyms *suffering* and *tribulation* appear in your study this week? What did you learn from marking these words?

If you are in a class setting and have access to a whiteboard, an overhead projector, or can put up "Write-On Cling Sheets"* and write on them, list insights as people share. Visual aids are a real asset in teaching, as the very

---

* Write-On Cling Sheets may be purchased at office supply stores. They are large sheets of white plastic which can be written on with dry-erase markers as you would write on a whiteboard. They are designed to adhere to walls simply by smoothing them over the surface of the wall. They do not damage wall surfaces. No tape or tacks are required to keep Write-On Cling Sheets in place. If you cannot find these locally, you may order them from Precept Ministries International by calling Customer Service at (800) 763-8280.

seeing of what is being said and discussed aids the memory. Ask the 5 W's and an H:

a. **Who** suffered or was afflicted?
b. **What** was the reason they suffered?
c. **When** did their affliction, suffering, or tribulation occur? **Where?**
d. **Why** did they suffer?
e. **How** were they afflicted, or how did they suffer?

∾ Now review every reference to the Lord's *coming* and list observations. (Again examine the references in the light of the 5 W's and an H.) You might ask questions like these:

a. Who is involved in His coming?
b. What do you learn about the Son?
c. Where will we, believers, be at His coming?
d. What will we be like at His coming?

∾ Take time to think through the general content of each chapter of 1 Thessalonians chapter by chapter. Again, list your insights.

∾ Did you notice the "break" in the context of the book? What happens at chapter 4? What change in direction or subject do you note in this epistle (letter)?

∾ What did you learn as a result of this week's lesson?

THOUGHT FOR THE WEEK

You—sanctified entirely! Set apart for God, holy in spirit, soul, and body! It's an awesome thought, isn't it? Especially in the light of the coming of our Lord Jesus Christ!

Wouldn't it be wonderful to have the confidence to know that when you stand before the Lord Jesus Christ to give an account of your life (and we all will stand before Him) that you will be able to stand there without blame...unashamed?

Do you realize, my friend, how Jesus Christ prayed for you just before He was arrested, taken to an illegal trial, and convicted and given over to crucifixion? He prayed, "I do not ask You to take them out of the world, but to keep them from the evil one. They are not of the world, even as I am not of the world. Sanctify them in the truth; Your word is truth. As You sent Me into the world, I also have sent them into the world. For their sakes I sanctify Myself, that they themselves also may be sanctified in truth" (John 17:15-19).

Won't you make it your goal, beloved child of God, to be the answer to your Lord's prayer?

*W*HAT'S *H*APPENED
*S*INCE *Y*OU *B*ELIEVED

~~~~

Do you remember the day you turned from walking your own way in order to serve the true and living God? Since then do you live in anticipation of the coming of God's Son who delivers you from the wrath to come? We should, Beloved; it's a purifying hope.

DAY ONE

Read 1 Thessalonians 1:1-7 and mark every reference to the Thessalonians, who are the recipients of this letter from Paul. Be sure to mark all of the pronouns *you* or *your* that refer to the Thessalonians. Also mark any synonyms that refer to them, such as *beloved* or *brethren*. (You may want to use the same color to mark the recipients of each epistle you study in the New Testament. I use orange.)

Now, make a list in your notebook entitled RECIPIENTS. Be sure to leave a page or two of space for this list as you will want to add to it throughout your study. Review every reference you marked and make a list of what you learn just from these seven verses. (You may not want to mark these references to recipients in your Bible, which is fine. If this is the case, simply add your insights to this list as you come to them in your study.) As you compile your list, you will find it helpful to note the chapter and verse from which your insight was gleaned. For instance, your observation list might look like this:

RECIPIENTS

1. Grace and peace to them (1:1)
2. Paul, Silvanus, and Timothy thank God always for them, and mention them in their prayers (1:2)
3. They (P-S-T) remember:
    their work of faith
    their labor of love
    their steadfastness of hope in the Lord Jesus
        Christ (1:3)

While this practice may seem a little tedious, it allows you to see and learn more than you would from simply reading the text. Writing down your observations and then thinking about what you have written is a great learning device. Also if you will read aloud what you write, you will be able to remember and recall the facts you are recording even more accurately.

DAY TWO

Yesterday as you compiled your insights on the Thessalonians, you saw that the Thessalonians "received the word in much tribulation." To help you better understand the significance of this statement, let's spend the next few days in the book of Acts.

Paul met the Thessalonians on his second missionary journey. The record of this journey begins in Acts 15:36. Although the account of Paul's arrival in Thessalonica is not recorded until Acts 17:1, read Acts 15:35–16:40 in order to get the big picture. As you read, do two things:

1. Trace Paul's second missionary journey on the map on page 42.

2. Note when and how both Silvanus (Silas) and Timothy join Paul on this journey. Record your insights in your notebook, along with any additional information you glean from the text concerning either of these men.

DAY THREE

Continue reading about Paul's second missionary journey in Acts 17:1-15. Then read Acts 18:1-11. As you read:

1. Mark each reference to time in a distinctive way. (You might want to use the symbol of a clock as was suggested in "How to Get Started.")

2. Continue to trace Paul's journey on the map on page 42.

3. Note when and where Silas (Silvanus) and Timothy separate from Paul.

4. Note where and when Silas and Timothy rejoin Paul.

DAY FOUR

As you begin today, make space in your notebook for a list entitled PAUL, SILAS, AND TIMOTHY IN THESSA-LONICA.

Read Acts 17:1-15; 18:1-11 again. Record all you learn about the time these men spent in Thessalonica. Leave ample space to add to this list throughout your study. Be sure to note how long they stayed, what was in Thessalonica, what they did during their time there, who they reached, what happened as a result, how they happened to leave Thessalonica, where they went next, what happened once they arrived at their next location, when they separated, when and where they each rejoined, and how long they...or Paul specifically...remained.

DAY FIVE

Read 1 Thessalonians 1 and mark the remaining references to the Thessalonians in this chapter. Add what you learn to the list you started in your notebook on Day 1.

Now, review your list on the Thessalonians and think about what you learned from your three-day study of the first portion of Paul's second missionary journey. How does what you learned from Acts fit with Paul's words to the Thessalonians in 1 Thessalonians 1? In your notebook, write out how the passage in Acts 17 explains what is recorded in 1 Thessalonians 1:6 regarding how they received the word. Also, look at the map on page 42 and note where the news of their conversion spread and why.

By the way, the account of Paul's third missionary journey begins in Acts 18:23. Look at the chart, SEQUENCE OF EVENTS IN PAUL'S LIFE AFTER HIS CONVERSION on pages 30-31. Note when 1 and 2 Thessalonians were written. It is believed that Paul wrote these epistles (letters) from Corinth.

DAY SIX

Before you go any further today, add the following key words to your bookmark and mark them the same way you will mark them in your Bible.

gospel (Mark any synonyms which would be references to the gospel.)

faith (Also mark *believe* if believe refers to believing God or believing the gospel. The English transliteration of the Greek* word for faith is the noun *pistis*, while the verb form believe is *pisteuō*.

love

hope

Holy Spirit[6]

Also mark references to *God the Father* and to *Jesus Christ*. (Special note: Because there can be so many references to God, Jesus, and the Holy Spirit, marking all references sometimes becomes too extensive. Therefore, mark only the references to God and Jesus that will help you remember or see something significant about the Father or the Son. For example, mark any reference that reveals a distinct part of Their character, Their ways, or Their will. However, it is wise to always mark all references to the Holy Spirit since there is so much erroneous teaching about the Spirit. Marking references to the Spirit helps readily identify all that the Scriptures teach about the Holy Spirit.) You will want to look for words on your bookmark throughout your study of 1 Thessalonians.

Today read back through chapter 1 again and mark these and any other key words noted on your bookmark that you may have overlooked earlier. Also be sure to look for any new insights into the Thessalonians and record these on your list, along with the chapter and verse.

---

* From time to time we will look at the definition of a word in the Greek. Since the New Testament was originally written in Koine Greek, sometimes it is helpful to go back to the Greek to see the original meaning of a word. We will always use the English transliteration of a Greek word, using the English equivalents for the Greek letters. There are many study tools to help you if you would like to do this type of digging. One excellent book to help you understand how to do more in-depth study is *How to Study Your Bible* (Harvest House Publishers, 1994).

Sequence of Events in Paul's Life After His Conversion*

*There are differing opinions on these dates. For continuity's sake this chart will be the basis for dates pertaining to Paul's life.

Scripture	Year A.D.	Event
Acts 9:1-25	33-34	Conversion, time in Damascus
	35-47	Some silent years, except we know that Paul:
Galatians 1:17		1. Spent time in Arabia and Damascus ⎤ 3 years
Acts 9:26; Galatians 1:18		2. Made first visit to Jerusalem ⎦
Acts 9:30–11:26; Galatians 1:21		3. Went to Tarsus, Syria-Cilicia area
Acts 11:26		4. Was with Barnabas in Antioch
Acts 11:30	44	5. With Barnabas took relief to brethren in Judea, and Paul's second visit to Jerusalem Herod Agrippa I dies
Acts 12:23		
Acts 12:25	47-48	6. Returned to Antioch; was sent out with Barnabas by church at Antioch
Acts 13:4–14:26		**First missionary journey:** *Galatians written (?)* Proconsul Sergius Paulus on Paphos is datable
Acts 15:1-35; Galatians 2:1	49	Apostolic Council at Jerusalem Paul visits Jerusalem (compare Acts 15 with Galatians 2:1)
	49-51	**Second missionary journey:** *1 and 2 Thessalonians written —1½ years in Corinth, Acts 18:11*
Acts 15:36–18:22	51-52	Gallio known to be proconsul in Corinth

14 years, Galatians 2:1 (spanning 35-47 to 47-48)

Scripture	Year A.D.	Event
Acts 18:23—21:17	52-56	**Third missionary journey:** *1 and 2 Corinthians and Romans written* — probably from Ephesus
Acts 21:18-23	56	Paul goes to Jerusalem and is arrested; held in Caesarea
Acts 24—26	57-59	Appearance before Felix and Drusilla; before Festus, appeals to Caesar; before Agrippa—datable
Acts 27—28:15	59-60	Went from Caesarea to Rome
Acts 28:16-31	60-62	First Roman imprisonment: *Ephesians, Philemon, Colossians, and Philippians written*— 2 years in prison
	62	Paul's release; possible trip to Spain
	62	Paul in Macedonia: *1 Timothy written*
	62	Paul goes to Crete: *Titus written*
	63-64	Paul taken to Rome and imprisoned: *2 Timothy written*
	64	Paul is absent from the body and present with the Lord *(Others put Paul's conversion about A.D. 35, his death at A.D. 68.)*

As you read chapter 1, you should see several simple lists. There is a list of three things in verse 3 that you don't want to miss, and another list is given in verse 5 when we are told how the gospel came. You can note simple lists right in the text of your Bible in this way: "constantly bearing in mind your ①work of faith and ②labor of love and ③steadfastness of hope in our Lord Jesus Christ in the presence of our God and Father."

DAY SEVEN

Store in your heart: 1 Thessalonians 1:5.
Read and discuss: 1 Thessalonians 1:1-10; Acts 15:36–16:40; 17:1-15.

QUESTIONS FOR DISCUSSION OR INDIVIDUAL STUDY

∾ Can you quote 1 Thessalonians 1:5 from memory? Note who is being quoted in this verse, and to whom he is speaking.

According to 1 Thessalonians 1:5, how did the gospel come? If you are in a class setting, write the five items in list form on the board as someone quotes the verse:

The Gospel Came In:
   1.
   2.
   3.
   4.
   5.

∾ Think back through the remaining verses of 1 Thessalonians 1, and note what happened as a result of verse 5.

ᇮ Review the passages in Acts listed under "Read and discuss." What do you observe in these verses that sub-
stantiates 1 Thessalonians 1:5 and the way the gospel
came to the Thessalonians? According to what you
studied in Acts, what do you observe in the lives of
Paul, Silas, and Timothy that would support this?

ᇮ Read 1 Thessalonians 1:6-8 and note the words "imitators" (verse 6) and "example" (verse 7).

If you are in a class setting and if time allows, ask various members of the class to share an insight they
recorded about the Thessalonians from chapter 1. As
each person shares, ask the class how what is being
read is an example to them today and if it is worthy of
imitation. If the class decides that it is an example to
be followed, ask how they might put this insight into
practice.

ᇮ What happened in your life this week as you studied?

THOUGHT FOR THE WEEK

Since you responded to the gospel of Jesus Christ, has
your life changed so that you are an example to others? Is
the Word of God now sounding forth from you to other
people wherever you go? Are you living your life in such a
way, my friend, that others are aware that you serve the
living and true God? Or haven't you yet utterly destroyed
the "idols" you once served?

Remember, Beloved, no man, woman, teen, or child can
serve two masters. Jesus Christ is God, and He alone is to be
served...no matter the tribulation, no matter the suffering,
no matter the affliction. God will not share His glory with
another, nor will He tolerate half-hearted obedience. He is

to be loved and served with all your heart, soul, mind, strength, and body.

God's Son is coming again. And when He comes, His reward will be with Him to give to every individual according to his deeds (Revelation 22:12). Your deeds are a manifestation of what you truly believe. Never forget that. Don't be deceived. He "gave Himself for us to redeem us from every lawless deed, and to purify for Himself a people for His own possession, zealous for good deeds" (Titus 2:14). May you "serve [the] living and true God" and "wait for His Son from heaven, whom He raised from the dead, that is Jesus, who rescues us from the wrath to come" (1 Thessalonians 1:9,10).

HOW DO YOU DELIVER THE GOSPEL IN AN EXEMPLARY WAY?

∾ ∾ ∾ ∾

If others were to imitate your life, would the result be for their good and God's glory?

DAY ONE

Read 1 Thessalonians 2. As you read, be sure to note whom this chapter focuses on. It will probably help you to see the focus if you mark every reference to "these" people in the same color. When you finish, record and complete the following statement in your notebook: "The main focus of this chapter is _____." Then note why you think this chapter's main focus is on these people. Why do you think the author is writing this chapter? Explain your response as you write.

DAY TWO

Read 1 Thessalonians 2 again and add to your list everything you learn from this chapter about the trio, Paul, Silvanus (Silas), and Timothy. As you record your insights, note what you learn from your observations. Interrogate the text by asking the 5 W's and an H. Note to whom they spoke the gospel, in what manner they spoke, how they behaved, why they spoke and behaved as they did, what they were *not* seeking, and what their goal was for those who heard. Also as you read, note and put in list form how reading Acts 16–17 put you into context with what is being said in 1 Thessalonians 2:1,2.

When you finish your list, stop and meditate on what you have observed. How, Beloved, do you measure up to the example of Paul, Silvanus, and Timothy?

DAY THREE

Read through 1 Thessalonians 2 and mark any key words listed on your bookmark. Stop and think about what you learn from marking each key word. Then add any new insights you gained about the recipients from this chapter to your running list on the Thessalonians.

Tomorrow we will look at the gospel in greater depth.

DAY FOUR

Today make a list in your notebook entitled THE GOSPEL. Leave adequate space in your notebook to add to the list as you continue your study, then note all that chapters 1 and 2 have to say about the gospel. Go back and look at every place you marked *gospel*. List the insights you gain from reviewing these. Although the word *gospel* is not used specifically in 1 Thessalonians 2:13, don't miss what this verse has to say about the gospel.

DAY FIVE

The apostle Paul gives a clear definition of the gospel in his first epistle to the Corinthians. Read 1 Corinthians 15:1-11 and mark the word *gospel* in the same way that you are marking it in 1 Thessalonians. Don't miss marking synonyms and pronouns that refer to the gospel as you read. You may also want to underline the repeated phrase, *according to the Scriptures.* Add to your list on the gospel any new insights you gleaned out of 1 Corinthians.

According to 1 Corinthians 15:1-8, what are the main points that you would want to make sure you cover if you share the gospel with another person? Be sure to list these in your notebook.

DAY SIX

Compare what you observed about the gospel yesterday in 1 Corinthians 15 with what Paul says in Romans 1:16 and 10:8-15. As you read these passages, watch the words *salvation* and *saved.* In your notebook, record your insights from Romans 1:16 and 10:8-15 under your list on the gospel. From these verses, note on your list who is saved, how they are saved, what it is necessary to believe, and what it is necessary to confess. Also note what happens when you do believe and confess.

When discussing the gospel, it is also insightful to consider what you are saved from. Therefore, look up the following verses, list them in your notebook under your list on the gospel, and next to each reference either record the verse in its entirety or the essence of the verse which shows what a person is saved from.

1. Romans 6:23
2. John 3:16
3. Colossians 1:13,14

DAY SEVEN

 Store in your heart: 1 Thessalonians 2:3,4.
Read and discuss: 1 Thessalonians 2:1-13.

QUESTIONS FOR DISCUSSION OR INDIVIDUAL STUDY

∽ Who is the main focus of 1 Thessalonians 2? Who do the authors talk about the most in this chapter? Why do you think they speak of these individuals?

∽ What did you learn from this chapter about how the gospel was delivered to the Thessalonians by Paul, Silvanus, and Timothy?

• Note the circumstances under which the gospel was shared. Compare these circumstances with your insights from last week's study of Acts.

• Note the motives and the integrity of those who presented the gospel. What did it cost them to share the gospel?

• Note too how Paul uses the illustration of a mother, then of a father.

• What do you learn about the expected behavior of mothers and fathers from these verses?

• What was Paul, Timothy, and Silvanus' goal for the Thessalonians?

Discuss all of these questions and then compare your insights with how the gospel is shared today by individuals and churches over television and radio. What might be things to look for when it comes to supporting those who claim to be sharing the gospel? Does this chapter offer any guidelines?

∾ Paul wrote that the trio's exhortation of the gospel did not come from error, impurity, or by way of deceit. He assures those to whom he is writing that they delivered what had been entrusted to them. So what is the gospel? If you were going to share the gospel with someone, what would you share? What truths would you need to impart? What did you discover in your study of 1 Corinthians 15:1-11? List the points of the gospel.

If you are in a class setting and if there is time, ask several in the class to share about the last time they shared the gospel with someone—what they said and how they presented the gospel.

∾ Review what you learned about salvation from Romans 6:23; John 3:16; and Colossians 1:13,14.

∾ Finally, what did you learn this week that really spoke to your heart?

THOUGHT FOR THE WEEK

When Paul, Silvanus, and Timothy delivered the gospel to those in Thessalonica, they did so in such a way that the new converts in Thessalonica first became imitators of them. Then as the converts grew in their relationship to the Lord Jesus, they became imitators of Jesus, which is as it should be.

In imitating Paul, Silvanus, Timothy, and then the Lord, their lives were so transformed that the Thessalonian believers became an example to all the believers in Macedonia and Achaia—and even further.

When you deliver the gospel to others, what is your life modeling? Is your message clear, biblical, free from ulterior motives, pure in its purpose and content? Is it delivered in a way and from a lifestyle that would win God's approval? Are you as gentle as a nursing mother, cherishing those given to you as a mother would care for her child? Are you exhorting, encouraging, imploring the lost and the newly born as a father would his own children? What kind of an example are you passing on to those who come to know Christ because of your witness? Are you even sharing the gospel with others?

How has God spoken to you this week, Beloved? What must you do to respond in obedience? Whatever it is, do it so that you can say with Paul, "I did not prove disobedient to the heavenly vision" (Acts 26:19).

WHAT PLACE HAS SUFFERING IN THE LIFE OF A CHILD OF GOD?

Are you wrestling with temptation, Beloved? Don't yield! There is more at stake than you realize.

DAY ONE

Read 1 Thessalonians 2:14–3:13 and note the flow of thought. Be sure to see how chapter 3 ties in with chapter 2. Take notice of Paul, Timothy, and Silvanus' concern for the Thessalonians. As you read, also underline every reference to Timothy. Keep in mind too the historical background you gained from reading Acts 17.

Glance over the map PAUL'S SECOND MISSIONARY JOURNEY on page 42 and note where Paul stayed after he left Thessalonica and before his arrival in Corinth. Trace his journey on the map on page 42. Refer to 1 Thessalonians 3:1,2 to see where Paul and Silas were left behind. This exercise will give you a chronological perspective on when Timothy was sent back to Thessalonica. When you finish reading, list the order of events laid out in 1 Thessalonians 2:14–3:11 in your notebook.

Paul's Second Missionary Journey

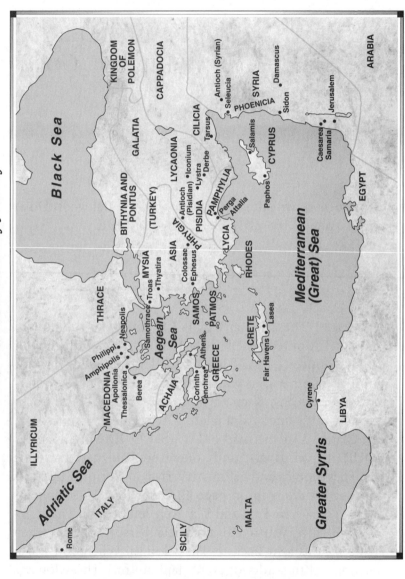

DAY TWO

Read 1 Thessalonians 3 and mark every reference to the Thessalonians. Note what you learn from chapter 3 about the Thessalonians in your notebook. Be certain to note what the Thessalonians' firm continuance in the faith will mean to Paul, Silvanus, and Timothy.

Beloved, who introduced you to Christ? Who nurtured you in the faith? Have you been tempted to turn away, to give in or give up? What do you think your faithfulness means to the one(s) who brought you to Christ?

What have you learned from this week's study that you can apply to your own life? Record your insights in your notebook. Also write out how God has spoken to you and record your intentions. Writing is good mental exercise, and what is cemented in your mind by it will serve as a reminder in the days ahead.

DAY THREE

Read through 1 Thessalonians 3 again and mark any key words from your bookmark.

Now compile in your notebook a list of what you learned from marking *affliction(s)*[7] and *suffer* in the first three chapters. As you make your list, think about this question: Was suffering experienced only by those in Thessalonica?

Now read 1 Thessalonians 2:14-16 again. Note where the suffering of the others mentioned in this passage came from and how their suffering compared with that of the authors and with that of the Thessalonians.

Look up Philippians 1:27-30 and 2 Timothy 3:12 to see what these Scriptures teach in respect to suffering. Both of these references are in letters written by Paul. Put your observations in your notebook under your list on suffering.

DAY FOUR

Read through 1 Thessalonians 1–3 again, noting where you marked every occurrence of *faith* and *believe*. Then as a review, list in your notebook what you learn from marking these words.

You may have already observed this, but just in case you haven't, let me ask you: According to 1 Thessalonians 2:13, what does the Word of God do in the lives of those who believe? From all you have studied of the text, do you think this "work" can be seen or noticed in any way? Record your insights in your notebook. The very process of writing down your thoughts will help crystallize and organize them.

Now, read 1 Corinthians 15:1,2 and note how what Paul says in these verses compares with his concern that the Thessalonian believers hold fast to their faith in the face of affliction.

Finally, read 1 John 2:18,19. What do these verses reveal to you about those who don't continue in the faith but turn and go out from among the believers? Record your insights in your notebook.

DAY FIVE

Read through 1 Thessalonians 2:17–3:13 again. This time mark every reference to *Satan*, along with any synonyms (i.e., *tempter*). You can mark references to the devil and his demons with a red pitchfork like this: **Satan**. This symbol makes the references very easy to spot.

Now make a list with the heading SATAN in your notebook and note everything you learn from this passage about him, the tempter.

Now then, do you think there is any association between Satan, the Thessalonians' afflictions, and Paul, Silvanus, and Timothy's concern regarding their faith? Record your answer and your reasoning in your notebook.

DAY SIX

Today we will take a deeper look at some other Scriptures about Satan. Turn to the following verses and record what you learn in your notebook:

1. The first mention of the devil is in Genesis 3:1-5 where he is referred to as the serpent. However, Revelation 12:9 and 20:2 clearly show that the serpent and the devil (or Satan) are one and the same. Read Genesis 3:1-5 and record on your list what you learn from these verses about Satan.

2. Notice the serpent's attitude toward what God has said, his subtle accusations regarding God, and what he tempts the woman to do. (The consequence of Adam and Eve's disobedience was death. Compare this with Romans 5:12.)

3. John 8:44 (Note to whom Jesus is speaking.)
4. Luke 22:31,32

DAY SEVEN

 Store in your heart: 1 Thessalonians 3:3,4.
Read and discuss: 1 Thessalonians 2:17–3:10.

QUESTIONS FOR DISCUSSION OR INDIVIDUAL STUDY

∾ Trace the course of events laid out in 1 Thessalonians
2:14–3:10, noting who went to which destination and
why. Include from 3:10,11 what Paul, Silvanus, and
Timothy are anticipating.

∾ What did you learn about afflictions and the Christian
from your study of the first three chapters of 1 Thessalonians?

   a. Who is going to suffer affliction? In answering this
   question, also consider the other verses you looked
   up from Philippians and 2 Timothy.

   b. Who is behind affliction?

   c. What kind of affliction did Paul, Silvanus, and
   Timothy suffer? Where did it come from?

   d. What kind of affliction did the Thessalonians suffer?
   In 1 Thessalonians 2:14,15 who also endured similar
   suffering?

   e. What do you learn about those who inflict this kind
   of suffering?

   f. What was Paul, Silvanus, and Timothy's concern in
   respect to the Thessalonians, their suffering, and
   their faith?

   g. Had they taught the Thessalonians anything in
   respect to suffering? If so, what? Look at Acts 17:2
   and note how long Paul was in Thessalonica.

h. From the verses you studied this week, do you think the Thessalonians stood firm in the face of affliction? What would you surmise as to the genuineness of their conversion? Support your answer with Scripture.

∾ What did you learn this week about Satan, his titles, and his tactics? Review what you recorded in your notebook.

∾ Finally, what was the most significant thing you studied, learned, or had reaffirmed this week?

THOUGHT FOR THE WEEK

If you live a life of genuine faith, Beloved, you can know for certain that in some way, some form, you *will* suffer affliction. No believer is granted exemption from suffering. It is a confirmation of the genuineness of your faith.

Paul, Silvanus, and Timothy had become anxious over the status of the Thessalonians. Their comfort came when Timothy returned to them bearing the good news of the faith and love of their Thessalonian converts and relaying the fact that the Thessalonians thought kindly of them. Their labor had not been in vain. The tempter had not succeeded. The Thessalonians had passed the test!

The good news of the Thessalonians' enduring faithfulness gave Paul, Silvanus, and Timothy the assurance that the believers at Thessalonica would be their hope, their joy, and their crown of exultation because they would be with them in the very presence of the Lord Jesus Christ at His coming. Paul, Silvanus, and Timothy really lived because the Thessalonians stood firm in the Lord.

Oh, yes, there was still room for growth in their faith, but Paul, Silvanus, and Timothy would complete "their faith" when they all were together once again. There was still room for the Thessalonians to increase in their love for one another, as is true for all men, but they were on their way. The labor of God's three ambassadors had not been in vain. What joy such knowledge brought them!

What about you, my friend? What do you do when you are tempted to turn away, to give in, or to give up because of the pressure? The affliction? The cost of obedience? Do you stop to think of those who introduced you to Christ? Of those who nurtured you in the faith?

What would your unfaithfulness do to them and to those who know your testimony? What reproach would you bring upon the name of our precious Lord Jesus Christ?

Is a moment of temporal acceptance from the world, temporal ease, joy, or pleasure worth the cost? No, Beloved, it could never be! Eternity is an awfully long time.

When we are tempted...when we get weary from the battle...when the tempter whispers in our ears, we must remember those who introduced us to Christ, those who nurtured us. We must think of how unfaithfulness on our part would affect others. Then, thinking clearly, we will choose to press on toward the prize of the high calling in Jesus.

Run, Beloved, run! The finish line is just ahead. Jesus is coming!

SEXUAL PURITY—HOW IMPORTANT IS IT?

～⌒～⌒～⌒～⌒

Are you having a problem with purity? Purity of mind? Of body? Do you think that "surely God understands"? Of course, He understands. However, although He understands, He will not tolerate immorality because He has given us a way of escape from such temptation.

DAY ONE

Today turn to the 1 THESSALONIANS AT A GLANCE chart on page 67 and look it over. Once the chart for a book is filled out, it provides a ready and pertinent overview for that book of the Bible. At a glance, you are able to discern points of vital information: who wrote the book, to whom it was written, the purpose and theme of the book, what material is covered in the book, and how the material is laid out chapter by chapter and segment by segment. The completed chart is an instant reference resource for future information and for discipling others. That is why *The New Inductive Study Bible* is such an asset. Therefore, fill in the chart in your *NISB* as well as in this book.

After four weeks of study and a thorough observation of the first three chapters of Thessalonians, it is now time

to fill in a portion of the 1 THESSALONIANS AT A
GLANCE chart. Before you go any further, let's talk for a
moment about chapter themes. To discover the theme of a
chapter, determine the main subject of that chapter by
looking at what topics are discussed most frequently in the
chapter and by noting what is emphasized or repeated
most often. A chapter theme will be easily remembered if it
meets the following criteria:

1. The theme should capture the essence of the main
subjects or events covered in that chapter.

2. The theme should be comprised of words actually
used in the text of the chapter.

3. Each chapter theme should be distinctive from the
others.

4. The theme should be as short and concise as possible.

Now then, following these guidelines, identify and fill
in the themes for chapters 1–3 on the 1 THESSALONIANS
AT A GLANCE chart. Also fill in any other portion of the
chart you are ready to complete. By the way, an acceptable
date for 1 Thessalonians is A.D. 51, so you can fill this information in on your chart too.

At this time, also note any "LFL" that is applicable for
you. Put your "LFL" in the margin of your Bible next to the
verse that the lesson is drawn from. Also record in your
notebook any "LFL" that you discovered in the first three
chapters of 1 Thessalonians.

DAY TWO

Read 1 Thessalonians 3:11–4:18. As you read, you will
notice a change in the content and tone of this letter. (We
discussed this in Week One.) Note where the change occurs

and what takes place at this point. This marks a segment division in the book. A segment division is a major division in a book. It is a group of verses or chapters that deal with the same subject, doctrine, person, place, or event.

What does the first segment of 1 Thessalonians dwell on or cover? Record your observations in your notebook under your notes on chapter 4. If you are comfortable with what you have seen, record it on your 1 THESSALONIANS AT A GLANCE chart in the segment division for chapters 1–3. Put a line between chapters 3 and 4.

Look at 1 Thessalonians 4:1. What does it seem that the author is going to deal with from this point on? Record your insights in your notebook, but don't fill in the portion of your AT A GLANCE chart that correlates to this segment yet. You will be able to complete the chart more easily once you finish reading chapter 5.

DAY THREE

Read through 1 Thessalonians 4:1-12 and mark key words from your bookmark. As you read, pay close attention to the author's transition in these verses from one subject to another.

Record in your notebook the subject that is covered in each of the paragraphs you read (4:1-8,9-12,13-18). When you finish, take a closer look at 1 Thessalonians 4:1-8. Read this paragraph again and be sure you marked every reference to the recipients. By the way, the verb *abstain* in 1 Thessalonians 4:3 is a present middle infinitive. The present tense indicates habitual and/or continuous action. The middle voice indicates that the subject participates in the action of the verb. Therefore, we are instructed *to keep on abstaining* from sexual lewdness and all forms of sexual sin. You are to be actively involved in practicing abstinence. God will meet you at your point of obedience.

Now add to your list everything you learn from marking the references to the Thessalonians. Then stop and think about what you have observed.

What have you seen about how you are to behave? How will the knowledge of what your behavior is to be impact your life? Do you need to make changes?

Finally, my friend, how are you going to live in the light of what you have seen?

DAY FOUR

Read through 1 Thessalonians 4:1-8 again. If you haven't been marking the references to God, it would be helpful to do so in this particular passage since it offers God's perspective on the Christian and his or her sexual purity or "sanctification." *Sanctification, sanctify, saint,* and *holy* all come from the same root word, which basically means "to be set apart." When you become a child of God, you become a saint in God's eyes—one who is set apart to Him and for Him. So before you move on to the next step, read and mark references to God. Then list in your notebook everything you learn about God in this passage.

The English transliteration of the Greek word for *sexual immorality* is *porneia.* It is also translated *fornication* and refers to lewdness or sexual sin. Sexual sin defiles. It brings uncleanness, impurity as 1 Thessalonians 4:7 says.

Let's look up some Scriptures which will give us additional insight into how God regards and deals with sexual immorality. Read Leviticus 20:7-16,23 (and Leviticus

20:17-22 if you have time). In your notebook, list the forms of sexual immorality mentioned in this passage. What are the consequences of participating in them?

Also look up Matthew 5:27-32; 1 Corinthians 6:9-11, 15-20; and Revelation 21:7,8 and record in your notebook the teaching in these passages regarding sexual immorality.

The Old and New Testaments contain many other passages on this topic, but time does not permit our study of them. However, what is laid out for us in 1 Thessalonians 4:1-8 is enough. Just remember what God says, "He who rejects *this* is not rejecting man but the God who gives His Holy Spirit to you" (1 Thessalonians 4:8).

DAY FIVE

Read 1 Thessalonians 4:9-18 marking the words *love*[8] and *hope.*

Now list in your notebook the specific instructions given by the authors to the Thessalonians in 4:9-12. Then think about these instructions. How are they being practiced in your life and in your church?

Now read 1 Thessalonians 1–4 and review every use of the words *love* and *hope.* Check the context of the uses and make a list in your notebook of what 1 Thessalonians teaches about love and about hope.

Take a personal inventory, asking yourself how you measure up.

DAY SIX

Finally, we come to a very interesting passage today. In many theological circles, this passage is referred to as the "rapture" passage. The word *rapture* is of Latin derivation and is taken from the Greek word *harpagēsometha,* which is translated "caught up" in 1 Thessalonians 4:17.

As you read 1 Thessalonians 4:13-18, note who is speaking, to whom they are speaking, what they are describing, and why. Watch for time phrases, such as *until, first,* and *then,*[9] which tell you when things will occur. Mark these with a little clock over the word since these words will help you understand the sequence of events described in this paragraph. Also note where people are, where they end up, and when and how all of this will be accomplished.

By the way, as you study this passage, the words *to meet* (verse 17) are *eis apantēsin* in the Greek text and mean "to come into the presence of, to meet."

Record your insights in your notebook, answering the 5 W's and an H posed above. If you have the time, do a stick drawing of the teaching of this passage. However, don't neglect your final assignment of this week in order to do it.

Compare 1 Thessalonians 4:13-18 with 1 Corinthians 15:51-54. First Corinthians 15:51-54 seems to be a parallel passage discussing the new bodies of those who are alive (do not sleep) and those who sleep. Study the passage and write out your observations in your notebook.

DAY SEVEN

Store in your heart: 1 Thessalonians 4:3,4 or 4:16,17. (Depending on your age and your need, memorize either of the suggested passages. You don't have to tell anyone which one you choose! However, you would be wise to commit both to memory!)

Read and discuss: 1 Thessalonians 4:1-8. When you finish, cover 1 Thessalonians 4:13-18.

QUESTIONS FOR DISCUSSION OR INDIVIDUAL STUDY

∽ What specific instructions are given in 1 Thessalonians 4:1-8? Consider what you learned about God in this chapter. Are there other things you have learned about God in this study that are pertinent to this week's study?

If you are in a class setting, record the insights shared in response to these questions on the board.

∽ What did you learn from the passages you studied which dealt with the subject of sexuality?

a. Leviticus 20:7-16,23

b. 1 Corinthians 6:9-11,15-20

c. Revelation 21:7,8

d. Matthew 5:27-32

∽ How can 1 Thessalonians 4:1-8 and the other verses you looked up on sexual immorality help in dealing with the issues of sexual immorality in the church and in our society?

∽ What insights did you gain from marking the word *love* in 1 Thessalonians?

∽ Think through 1 Thessalonians 4:13-18 by covering the 5 W's and an H.

a. What was the occasion of this subject?

b. What can you discern from the context as to the reason this subject was brought up?

   c. What does this passage teach about grief and about those who have no hope?

   d. What did you learn from marking *hope* in 1 Thessalonians? According to verse 14, if you believe in the resurrection, then you also need to believe what Paul is about to explain.

   e. Who is going to participate in this event?

   f. When will this event happen?

   g. What is the sequence of events?

   h. Where will it all take place?

   i. How is it going to happen?

∽ What did you learn from 1 Corinthians 15:51-54? Do you see any relationship between 1 Thessalonians 4:13-18 and 1 Corinthians 15:51-54? If so, what? How? Does this knowledge give you hope? Does it comfort you? How?

THOUGHT FOR THE WEEK

Although sexual immorality has been prevalent in every generation, it is clear from 1 Thessalonians and the other passages you studied that a lifestyle of sexual immorality in any form—heterosexual, homosexual, incestuous, or even mental—is unacceptable in Christianity.

Those who teach to the contrary can know that it is not the opinion or theology of man they reject, but that they have set themselves up against the clear Word of God. To twist God's Word, to rationalize God's Word on this subject of sexual immorality, is to summon God's vengeance. And it is a summons that God will surely answer. He has made it clear in His Word that no man is to "transgress and defraud his brother in the matter because the Lord is *the* avenger in all these things, just as we also told you before and solemnly warned *you*" (1 Thessalonians 4:6).

Whenever God calls you to a life of obedience, my friend, you can know that He always provides you with a way to obey. As God calls you to abstain from sexual immorality by possessing your own vessel (body) in sanctification and honor, He provides the means for your abstinence, moment by moment and temptation by temptation. This means is the power found in the gift of His Holy Spirit, who indwells every believer. It is by His Spirit that He provides us with the promised victory over the desires of the flesh. Victory is assured if we will simply walk by His Spirit and let His Spirit have control over our flesh (Galatians 5:16). If you are a child of God, you must abstain, Beloved. It is the will of God.

You: Sanctified Entirely— Body, Soul, and Spirit

Are you examining things carefully? Holding fast to what is good? Abstaining from every form of evil? Our Lord Jesus Christ is coming, Beloved. Surely you want to be without blame when you see Him face-to-face.

DAY ONE

Read 1 Thessalonians 5 to get a sense of how Paul brings this letter to a close. What are his final concerns? In general, what is covered in this chapter? Record your insights in your notebook.

DAY TWO

Read 1 Thessalonians 5:1-11 again and mark every reference to the Thessalonians. As you read, notice how the authors include themselves in what they are saying to the Thessalonians. Watch the words *we* and *us* in conjunction with the word *you.*

Add new observations to your list in your notebook.

DAY THREE

Now read 1 Thessalonians 5:1-11 a third time and mark the key words from your bookmark. You will notice that there is a key word (phrase) you haven't marked yet in your study of 1 Thessalonians, a new subject Paul has yet to deal with. Be sure to watch for and mark this key word and any appropriate synonyms or pronouns. This phrase signals a transition into another subject. What subject does the author cover in these verses? Record everything you learn about this event in your notebook.

DAY FOUR

When you read 1 Thessalonians 5:1-11, did you get the sense that Paul had already taught the Thessalonians about the *day of the Lord* (our new key phrase) even before he wrote this letter? From our look at Acts 17, we know that Paul spent at least three Sabbaths in Thessalonica. Because the Lord's coming is mentioned in every chapter of 1 Thessalonians, it is obvious this is a subject Paul taught the Thessalonians when he was with them.

If these subjects were covered with new believers who were suffering persecution because of their faith in the Lord Jesus Christ who someday would raise them from the dead (as Paul said in 4:13-18), how important do you feel this teaching is for our day?

Before we focus on *the day of the Lord,* let's look at the general subject of Jesus' coming. It will be good background for our three weeks in 2 Thessalonians. You don't want to miss this study either!

Carefully read 1 John 3:1-3 and write these verses out in your notebook. Then answer the following questions:

1. What hope is being discussed in these verses?

2. When will this hope be realized?

3. What does this hope cause us to do?

Now having studied 1 Thessalonians 4:13-18 and having read about *the day of the Lord* in chapter 5, let's go through 1 Thessalonians and take a fresh look at everything you can observe from the references to the Lord's coming you've marked throughout this epistle. First, take note of the fact that the English transliteration of the Greek word used for *coming* in 1 Thessalonians is *parousia*, which basically means "presence or arrival; to be present, to come to a place."

Go back now and look at each reference you marked and see what you can learn about the following. As you look at each reference, record your insights in your notebook.

1. Where will the people mentioned be?

2. Who is going to be with Him?

3. How do they get to be with Him?

4. What will they be like—what will be the status of body, soul, and spirit?

5. Who is coming with Him?

Now, compare what you saw in 1 John 3:1-3 with what you just reviewed from 1 Thessalonians. If this hope is a purifying hope, isn't that why the authors are eager that the Thessalonians be sanctified, without blame? Of course!

And the same is true for you, beloved student. Being in the Word of God, learning what it says, and obeying it is the way you, too, will be ready for that day and not ashamed when He comes.

DAY FIVE

As you read 1 Thessalonians 5:1-11 again today, watch for the author's contrast of the Thessalonians with another group. Note the *they* and the *them.* Be sure to note the contrast in verse 4. Mark every reference to this group in a distinctive way, and then list in your notebook what you observe from the text about this group.

From all you have observed from 1 Thessalonians 5:1-11, what do you think the believer's relationship is to the day of the Lord? Write out the reason for your answer.

Today we leave you to ponder this question. We will delve into the subject more thoroughly in our brief study of 2 Thessalonians.

DAY SIX

The remainder of 1 Thessalonians 5 is basically a series of exhortations and instructions. An exhortation is an encouragement. An instruction is a command. Read all of chapter 5 and mark any key words from your bookmark.

Although marking exhortations and instructions may seem tedious, you will find it beneficial to list these in your notebook. As you look at this chapter, give special attention to 1 Thessalonians 5:14. This verse tells you how you are to respond to three different "kinds" of individuals. Understanding this verse will give you wisdom in dealing with people. Once you have listed the exhortations and instructions, examine your own life and walk with the Lord in the light of these exhortations. You might want to put "LFL" or a star beside any exhortation or instruction that you feel you need to ask the Lord to incorporate into your life.

One last list! Remember that you marked references to the *Holy Spirit*.[10] So now go through the book of 1 Thessalonians and review the references to the Spirit and record what you learn from 1 Thessalonians about the Holy Spirit in your notebook.

Record the themes of chapters 4 and 5 on the 1 THESSALONIANS AT A GLANCE chart.

Finally, don't miss that wonderful statement of truth in 1 Thessalonians 5:24. Note its context.

DAY SEVEN

Store in your heart: 1 Thessalonians 5:15-18. How we need to know and live by these verses! If we really lived by them, can you imagine the impact we would have on a society that lives the antithesis of these verses?

Read and discuss: 1 Thessalonians 5:12-28. (We will study and discuss the day of the Lord in 2 Thessalonians.)

QUESTIONS FOR DISCUSSION OR INDIVIDUAL STUDY

∾ Review the exhortations and instructions given to the Thessalonians in the entire fifth chapter. Think of how they are to be lived out practically in day-to-day life. For instance, God tells us in verse 11 that we are to encourage one another, to build up one another. How is that being done in your family, in your church, in your place of business? Or how are you appreciating those who labor among you and have the spiritual oversight of the believers?

If you are in a class setting, ask the class to share which one of the exhortations spoke to them individually and why. Discuss the above questions as the class looks at each exhortation. If God's exhortation for us to rejoice always and "in everything give thanks; for this is God's will for you in Christ Jesus" (1 Thessalonians 5:18) sparks questions about how rejoicing in adverse circumstances is possible, look at God's promises which assure us that He is in control. It would be good to include Romans 8:28-30 in your discussion. Also compare 1 Thessalonians 5:18 with Ephesians 5:20.

What did you learn from 1 Thessalonians about the Holy Spirit? What does it mean to quench the Holy Spirit? There are basically five commands regarding the Holy Spirit:

a. Be filled with the Holy Spirit (Ephesians 5:18). Note verses 19,20 in relationship to being filled. Watch how verse 20 goes along with 1 Thessalonians 5:18.

b. Walk by the Spirit (Galatians 5:16).

c. Pray in the Spirit (Ephesians 6:18).

d. Do not grieve the Holy Spirit (Ephesians 4:30).

e. Do not quench the Holy Spirit (1 Thessalonians 5:19).

How does each command relate to your relationship with the Holy Spirit? (In a class setting, be certain that each person in the class realizes that if they are truly a child of God the Holy Spirit indwells them as stated in Ephesians 1:13,14.)

ᕇ What is the most significant thing you have learned in your study of 1 Thessalonians?

   a. What has happened to you personally through this study?

   b. What truth has been the hardest?

   c. What have you learned about studying the Bible?

THOUGHT FOR THE WEEK

Sanctified entirely—our spirit, our body, our soul all preserved complete and without blame when Jesus comes. It is an incredible thought, isn't it, Beloved? Do you think it could never be true of you because even though you know the willingness of your spirit, you also know the weakness of your flesh?

God knows what you know. He knows and fully understands the weakness of your flesh. Didn't Jesus tell the disciples in the Garden of Gethsemane to watch and pray because the spirit was willing but the flesh was weak? How did Jesus know? He too wrestled with the will of God when He prayed and asked the Father if it was possible to "remove this cup from me: nevertheless not my will, but thine, be done" (Luke 22:42 KJV). Three times Jesus went to the Father with the same request, the same prayer. You can rest assured, my friend, our Lord understands the weakness of our humanity.

Because Jesus experienced the weakness of the flesh firsthand, He told them to watch and pray. And this is why, Beloved, He tells us through Paul to "rejoice always; pray without ceasing; in everything give thanks; for this is God's will for you in Christ Jesus" (1 Thessalonians 5:16-18).

O Beloved, if we will do our part...if we will hear and obey His Word...if we will examine everything carefully, holding fast to what is good and abstaining from every form of evil, He will do His part by sanctifying us completely. We have His promise: "Faithful is He who calls you, and He also will bring it to pass" (1 Thessalonians 5:24).

Theme of 1 Thessalonians:

SEGMENT
DIVISIONS

		CHAPTER THEMES	Author:
	1		
			Historical Setting:
	2		
			Purpose:
	3		
			Key Words:
	4		
	5		

SECOND THESSALONIANS

INTRODUCTION TO 2 THESSALONIANS

Rumors can be destructive. They can shake our faith, rob us of peace, and steal away all joy...especially when they are the kind of rumors that portend a shaky and uncertain future.

Rumors can keep us from thinking clearly, rationally. They can cause us to forget truths we once held...truths which sustained and undergirded us.

Rumors can rock our confidence in the truths that give our lives stability and enable us to withstand life's storms and tempests. They can cause us to make wrong decisions, to base our lives in false realities that result in fear rather than confidence. They can keep us in a state of torment by raising constant questions related to our very survival.

How can we endure rumors? How can we survive the turmoil they create? The end result of rumors is that we can become deflated and simply give up. When we become overpowered by the fear of rumors, we cast ourselves adrift on the waves of circumstances to be tossed hither and yon, rather than charting our course and unflinchingly sailing through and beyond the storm into the safety of our chosen harbor.

The only way to handle and to quell rumors is to ascertain truth for yourself. And once you find it, you must stand on the fact that since truth *is* truth, it will never change. This is the stance the Thessalonians needed to take. It is where we all need to stand!

WHAT'S THE FATE OF THOSE WHO AFFLICT THE CHILD OF GOD?

DAY ONE

It had been four to six months since Paul wrote his first epistle to the church at Thessalonica. Now he's writing again. Why? Read through the book of 2 Thessalonians and see if you can discover his most urgent, most prevailing reason for writing this letter.

As you read, watch for any mention of distress among the believers and note the reason for their distress. If you see this reason on your first reading of 2 Thessalonians, record it in your notebook under 2 Thessalonians 1.

DAY TWO

You can use the same bookmark for this study that you used for your study of 1 Thessalonians. So read through 2 Thessalonians 1:1–2:2 and mark the key words from your bookmark. In your study of this book, mark *afflict(ed)*[11] and *affliction(s)*[12] in a different way than you mark *suffering*[13] and *persecutions.*

According to 2 Thessalonians 2:1,2, what had happened to the believers at Thessalonica? Why did it happen? Set up a place in your notebook to record general impressions just as you did for 1 Thessalonians and record your insights under 2 Thessalonians, chapter 1.

Now then, from what you learned about the day of the Lord in your study of 1 Thessalonians, do you think that the afflictions, the sufferings, and the persecutions the Thessalonian believers were undergoing might have made them more susceptible to the "rumor" that the day of the Lord had already come?

DAY THREE

Now that we have a general picture of this short epistle, let's see what we can learn from 2 Thessalonians 1. Read the first chapter and mark every reference to the recipients of this epistle. If you do not want to mark these references in your Bible, then simply record what you observe in your notebook. Either way, compile a list in your notebook of what you learn about the recipients.

As you review your list, note the way what you learn about the Thessalonians corresponds with Paul's previous commendations and desires for them. Compare 1 Thessalonians 3:5-10 and the comments regarding their faith with 2 Thessalonians 1:3,4. Then compare the comment on their love in 2 Thessalonians 1:3 with 1 Thessalonians 4:9,10. Record your observations in your notebook under chapter 1.

DAY FOUR

What can you learn about God and the Lord Jesus Christ from 2 Thessalonians 1? Read through the chapter again and mark every reference to *God* and to the *Lord Jesus (Christ)*. Also mark every reference to *glory*[14] and *glorified* in a distinctive way. Add these words to your bookmark.

Add any new insights from the text of chapter 1 about God and Jesus Christ to the list you began on Jesus and God in 1 Thessalonians.

Are you surprised by what you learn about God in this chapter? How do you think the world would respond if you shared these insights with them? What if they disagreed with you? What if they had heard something else about God and countered you with what they felt was true? Would that shake you? Why or why not?

DAY FIVE

As we saw in our study of 1 Thessalonians, it is the lot of Christians to suffer. According to 2 Thessalonians 1, when does relief come? How? Write your answer in your notebook in the form of a complete statement so that you will remember the questions you are answering. You might write something like this: "Relief from affliction, persecution, and suffering will come for the children of God when _____."

According to 2 Thessalonians 1, exactly what is going to happen to those who do not know the Lord and who afflict the children of God? Read through the chapter carefully, marking every reference to these people. Then make a list of everything you learn about them from this chapter. Examine your information in light of the 5 W's and an H. Although many of these questions overlap, you will want to ask questions like these:

- Who are these people? How are they described?

- What have they done? How have they related and/or responded to God?

• Where are they now? What will be done to them? By whom?

• Where will they be? For how long?

When you finish interrogating the text with the purpose of learning all you can about these people, record any new insights you glean from asking these questions.

DAY SIX

Identify and record the main theme of 2 Thessalonians 1 on the 2 THESSALONIANS AT A GLANCE chart on page 100.

This study of 2 Thessalonians will probably spark your interest in the mystery of what lies ahead, of what it will be like when God deals out retribution on all those who do not know Him and who do not obey the gospel of our Lord Jesus Christ. That, my friend, is what the book of Revelation is all about. If you want to know for yourself exactly what is going to transpire, we suggest you do four studies on Revelation in our Precept Upon Precept Bible study series.*

---

* If you want to do a more thorough and comprehensive study of the subject of the church in the end times and prophecy so that you can see for yourself what the Scriptures say, then order our inductive studies on Revelation. You probably will never do a more thorough, rewarding, or enlightening course. It is purely inductive. Although you will never touch a commentary, you will be absolutely awed at what you can see and learn on your own as you study the Word inductively. However, if this four-part series is beyond your time constraints, then there is an excellent 13-week study on Revelation, *Behold, Jesus Is Coming!,* in The New Inductive Study Series. It is part of the study series you are working through now. For information on this course, contact Precept Ministries International at 800-763-8280, visit our website at www.precept.org, or fill out and mail the response card at the back of this book.

Now then, what is your assignment for today? It is simply to read Revelation 14:14-16,19,20 just to get a sense of what it will be like when God deals out His retribution on those who do not believe on Him.

DAY SEVEN

Store in your heart: 2 Thessalonians 1:6,7.
Read and discuss: 2 Thessalonians 1:3–2:2.

QUESTIONS FOR DISCUSSION OR INDIVIDUAL STUDY

∾ What did you learn about the circumstances of those in Thessalonica at the time this second epistle was written?

∾ What do you think was Paul's primary reason for writing this second epistle?

∾ As you observed 2 Thessalonians 1, what did you learn about the Thessalonian believers? Discuss insights that can be applied to daily life. Does this chapter communicate a sense of hope or of despair for the believers?

∾ Ask the 5 W's and an H about those God will pay with affliction.

a. Who are these people? How are they described?

b. What have they done? How have they related and/or responded to God?

c. Where are they now? What will be done to them? By whom?

d. Where will they be? For how long?

∽ What do you learn about God and about Jesus Christ from this chapter?

∽ What are your general impressions of the passages you read from Revelation? How do these passages shed light on the retribution which will be dealt out by God on those who do not know Him and do not obey the gospel of the Lord Jesus Christ?

THOUGHT FOR THE WEEK

How many times have people cried out, "If God is God, then why doesn't He do something about all the injustice in the world? Why does He allow His children to suffer so? Why doesn't He come to the aid of those who belong to Him?"

He does, Beloved. He does! The people of this world just can't understand it because they don't know what it is to have "Christ in you, the hope of glory" (Colossians 1:27). Glory awaits us. We will be vindicated. The guilty will not go unpunished. God is just and righteous, Redeemer and Judge.

The present suffering we endure makes us worthy of the kingdom of God. Our steadfast and patient endurance, our perseverance in the face of persecution, suffering, and affliction testifies to the reality of our faith.

Press on, Beloved, so that our God may count you worthy of your calling and fulfill every desire for goodness and the work of faith with power, so that the name of our Lord Jesus may be glorified in you and you in Him, according to the grace of our God and the Lord Jesus Christ.

WHEN WILL THE
DAY OF THE LORD COME?

∾∾∾∾

Truth is liberating! But before you can be liberated, you need to know truth!

DAY ONE

Second Thessalonians 2 is a critical chapter to your understanding of prophecy. Therefore, you need to move through it carefully. Take time to observe the text thoroughly. Be sure to let the text itself convey its own message without drawing any premature conclusions or believing any preconceived ideas. This type of observation will be our task for this week.

Read all of today's instructions carefully before you begin. As you begin your observations, look for the "who's" of chapter 2, the main characters.

Glean everything you can about these people from the text. Make a chart in your notebook like the one on pages 98 and 99 called THE PERSONAGES OF 2 THESSALONIANS 2. It will be good to have the chart in your notebook where you will have more room to write should you need it. You can then transfer your insights to the chart in the book.

As you can see, this chart has five columns, THE THESSALONIANS, THE MAN OF LAWLESSNESS, THE

LORD JESUS CHRIST, HE WHO RESTRAINS, and THOSE WHO PERISH. Choose a distinctive color for each person and color the heading of the column on the chart with the same color you will use to color-code that personage in the text of your Bible. Of course, you will want to use the same color you have been using throughout this study for the Thessalonians.

Let's begin today with the recipients of this epistle. Read chapter 2 and mark every reference to the Thessalonian believers, the *brethren*,[15] as Paul calls them. Don't forget to mark all pronouns and synonyms. Then record your insights on your chart in your notebook.

Be sure to note Paul's concern and the reason he is concerned for them. What things has he taught them? What does he want them to understand?

When your assignment is complete, it would be good to read 2 Thessalonians 2 again to catch the flow of this chapter. You will see in verse 13 how he contrasts the Thessalonians with those who perish in verses 10-12. When you finish reading, check your chart to make sure it is complete. Think about what you have observed. Note the word *but* in verse 13 and the word *then*[16] in verse 15.

Review your chart to make sure you haven't missed anything, then transfer your final observations to the chart in this book.

DAY TWO

The next personage you want to observe is the *man of lawlessness*.[17] Carefully read the text and mark every synonym and pronoun used to describe him. Read the text carefully, watching the pronouns. Make certain you know to whom the pronouns refer before you mark them. When you finish, record your insights on the chart in your notebook and then on the chart on page 98.

An interesting parallel New Testament passage is Matthew 24:15-30. At the end of yesterday's lesson, you were instructed to notice the word *then*[18] in 2 Thessalonians 2:15. As you read these verses from Matthew, you will find it insightful to mark the word *when* in 24:15 and then draw a line connecting it with the other *thens*[19] in verses 16,21,23. (I circled them in green in my Bible and then drew a line from each one to the next, kind of like "connecting the dots.")

Next, mark the phrase *a great tribulation*[20] in verse 21. Then mark *immediately after the tribulation of those days*[21] (another time phrase) in verse 29. Finally, note *then*[22] in verse 30 where you see the announcement of the coming of our Lord Jesus. He is the Son of Man, whom we have been reading about in 1 and 2 Thessalonians!

When you finish, if you have time, review what you have written and think about what you have learned about the man of lawlessness. Recall what you observed with respect to his taking his seat in the temple of God. Note how this account parallels with the abomination of desolation standing in the holy place. Both places are the *naos,* a reference to the Holy of Holies in the Jewish temple. What does this tell you about the necessity of the presence of a literal temple at this time?

DAY THREE

Carefully read 2 Thessalonians 2:1-12 and mark every reference to the *Lord Jesus Christ* in the same way you marked the references to Him previously. Then record your insights on the chart in your notebook and then on the chart on page 99. Record your insights even if they overlap what you recorded about the Thessalonians or the man of lawlessness.

There are still two other "personages" to observe. One is mentioned in 2 Thessalonians 2:7, *he who now restrains*.[23] There is not a lot of information to observe, but what can be seen is critical because of the key role this restrainer plays in the scenario of events. Record your insights on "he who now restrains" in your notebook and on the chart on page 99.

Finally, let's look at the last personage. It is a group referred to as *those who perish*.[24] Beginning in verse 10, mark all references to this group, including pronouns, and record your insights on the charts. When you finish, compare your observations with what you observed about the Thessalonians in verses 13-17. There is an intended contrast by the author.

DAY FOUR

Today read all of the instructions before you begin. In today's study, you will take a thorough look at the day of the Lord as described in 2 Thessalonians 2. Read the chapter very carefully. Mark every reference to *the day of the Lord*[25] or *the coming of our Lord Jesus Christ*. Don't forget to mark the pronouns and synonyms. When you finish, read the chapter again and record in your notebook everything you learn from this chapter about this event.

Note what will precede the day of the Lord, the order of the events, and any impression you receive from this chapter as to the Thessalonians' anticipation of this day. Watch any time phrases such as *will not come unless*[26] and *then.*[27]

As you observe the day of the Lord in this chapter, consider the following: In verse 2 when it says "to the effect that the day of the Lord has come,"[28] the verb *has come*[29] is a perfect active indicative verb. The perfect tense of the verb *has come* would imply an action which took place in the past and remains true. The active voice means that the subject (the day of the Lord) performs the action. The indicative mood is the declarative mood or mood of certainty, a statement of fact which assumes reality from the speaker's point of view.

Now, in the light of this knowledge read the verse again in its context. Ask yourself what the Thessalonians are saying and what Paul is saying. You will get a better understanding of why Paul needed to write to them again so soon after writing his first epistle.

DAY FIVE

On page 97 you will find the chart WHAT 1 & 2 THESSALONIANS TEACH ABOUT THE DAY OF THE LORD. Take your study notes on the day of the Lord from 1 and 2 Thessalonians and compile them on this page. As you work, note any insights you can glean about this day by interrogating the text with the 5 W's and an H. You won't have all the answers on the day of the Lord, but it will be a good start. See how many of the following questions are answered in 1 and 2 Thessalonians:

1. Who will be present? Who will be absent? Who will be involved?

2. What do you know about that day?

3. When will it happen?

4. Where will it take place?

5. Why will it come?

6. How will it come or happen?

Once you finish your work, review your chart THE PER-
SONAGES OF 2 THESSALONIANS 2 to refresh your
memory as to how each of these people or groups of people
relate to the day of the Lord. Also remember to complete
your 2 THESSALONIANS AT A GLANCE chart on page 100
by recording your theme for chapter 2. Last, note any
"LFL's" you can apply.

DAY SIX

Today we are going to look up other references to the
day of the Lord to see what they say about this day. As
you look up these verses, record any new insights on the
chart in your notebook. You may also want to list the references to *the day of the Lord* in the margin of your Bible
next to 2 Thessalonians 2.

Remember to examine the references in their context.
Context is the verses that precede and follow the verse(s)
you are looking up. Also watch for the word *before* and
mark it in the text since it is a time phrase and critical to
understanding the timing of events in your observations.
Have fun, but don't assume you have a complete picture of
the day of the Lord! There is much more to study.

1. Joel 1:15; 2:1-3,11,30-32

2. Acts 2:14-21 (a reference to Joel 2)

3. Malachi 4:5,6

DAY SEVEN

 Store in your heart: 2 Thessalonians 2:3.
Read and discuss: 2 Thessalonians 2.

QUESTIONS FOR DISCUSSION OR INDIVIDUAL STUDY

∾ What did you learn about the different personages in
2 Thessalonians 2?

In a class setting, duplicate the chart the students made
in their study and record their insights. The repetition
of material and the ensuing discussion will help seal
the truths of 2 Thessalonians 2 to their minds.

As you look at the contrast between the Thessalonians
and those who perish, ask the class what they learned
about genuine Christianity from these lists. Note the
fact that the lost did not believe or love truth. As you
look at the man of lawlessness, note that he has power
and the ability to do signs and wonders. This fact
should help the class to realize that supernatural phe-
nomena do not necessarily verify an individual's cre-
dentials as godly. Just because we hear of signs and
wonders taking place or see them demonstrated in
person or on television, they alone do not substantiate
the genuineness of an individual's claim of doing the
work of God or of being sent from God.

*The fact that the class is doing this study shows a respect,
an appreciation, and even a love for the truth because
they are willing to seek it on their own and discipline
themselves for the purpose of godliness. Please congratu-
late them for us at Precept Ministries and tell them how*

much we appreciate them. Please know too that we are grateful for your leadership and for your willingness to lead them into truth.

∾ What did you learn about the day of the Lord? Make sure you remember the three things in 2 Thessalonians which must occur *before* the day of the Lord: the apostasy first (verse 3), the man of lawlessness is revealed (verse 3), and the restrainer is taken out of the way (verse 7). The removal of the restrainer has to precede the revelation of the man of lawlessness before the day of the Lord comes.

∾ Think through Matthew 24 to see what happens after the man of lawlessness, the abomination of desolation, takes his place in the temple. Follow the time phrases and you will see that the coming of the Lord follows all of this. What were the Thessalonians looking for? The day of the Lord or the coming of the Son of Man, their Lord Jesus Christ? Could the fact that Paul previously taught the Thessalonians that they would escape the day of the Lord, that they were not destined to go through its wrath, be the reason they were so distressed and so shaken? Could it be the reason they were so disturbed by a spirit, message, or letter as if from Paul, Silvanus, and Timothy announcing to them that the day of the Lord had already come? It is a question worth pondering, isn't it? Maybe because of what Paul had taught them they thought they would meet the Lord in the air before the day of the Lord and be with Him "at the coming of our Lord Jesus with all His saints" (1 Thessalonians 3:13). Maybe that's why Paul said, "with regard to the coming of our Lord Jesus Christ, *and* our gathering together (*episunagōgēs:* to assemble together) to Him."

THOUGHT FOR THE WEEK

Knowing the truth for ourselves is so very important, isn't it? If we know truth because of our own study, we won't be tossed about by every wind of doctrine and cunning craftiness of men by which they lie in wait to deceive us...or shaken from our composure...or disturbed with a revelation that is apart from the Word of God, His infallible Bible.

May you continue to love truth, to pursue it. May you continue to be an answer to our Lord's prayer for you: [Father,] I do not ask You to take them out of the world, but to keep them from the evil one" (John 17:15). Remember Satan is a liar, a deceiver, and does not abide in the truth. He is the one who will energize the man of lawlessness. Yet, Beloved, you do have an offensive weapon, the only one you need—the Word of God, the sword of the Spirit. And thus Jesus continued His prayer, "Sanctify them in the truth; Your word is truth" (John 17:17).

Take your sword from its sheath, kiss it, and go forward, valiant one! The victory is yours.

WHAT ABOUT THOSE WHO LEAD UNDISCIPLINED LIVES?

What does God have to say about an undisciplined life and an unruly lifestyle?

DAY ONE

Now we come to a change of pace and a change in the course of the teaching in this short epistle. Read 2 Thessalonians 3 simply to get the sense of the direction that Paul's letter now takes. Note the term he uses in verse 1 which alerts his readers that he is approaching the end of his letter. As you read, mark every occurrence of the words *model*[30] or *example.*[31] Then mark every reference to Paul, Silvanus, and Timothy. Also mark the pronouns *we* and *us*, as well as pronouns that refer to Paul. When you finish marking references to the authors, turn back to the first chapter of 1 Thessalonians and read it again.

In the light of all you have learned about Paul's primary purpose for writing this second letter to the Thessalonians, why do you think Paul puts his distinguishing mark on this letter? Record your insight in your notebook under 2 Thessalonians 3.

DAY TWO

Today read through chapter 3 and mark every reference to the Thessalonians. Then make a list in your notebook under your chapter 3 heading of everything you learn in this chapter from marking the references to the "trio." Also record Paul's purpose for writing what he does in this chapter.

DAY THREE

Add the word *undisciplined (unruly)*[32] to your bookmark. Then read through 2 Thessalonians 3 again and mark the key words from your bookmark. List what you learn about the "undisciplined" in your notebook.

When you finish compiling this list of your observations, read chapter 3 again to see if there is anything in this list that you personally relate to in any way. If so, indicate this in your notebook by putting a star by your observation and then talk to the Lord about it.

DAY FOUR

In 2 Thessalonians 3:1, Paul asks the Thessalonian believers to pray for them. Prayer was an integral part of Paul's ministry and life. Look up the following references to prayer in 1 and 2 Thessalonians. Write these references in your notebook. Under each reference write what you observe from the text about prayer. Examine these verses and the subject of prayer in the light of the 5 W's and an H.

1. 1 Thessalonians 1:2-5
2. 1 Thessalonians 3:9-13
3. 1 Thessalonians 5:17,18,25
4. 2 Thessalonians 1:11,12
5. 2 Thessalonians 3:1,2

As you look at Paul's request for prayer in 2 Thessalonians 3:1,2, you will see a reference to *the evil one.* There is some question about this translation because it could simply be *from evil* or *from the evil one.* Go back to 1 Thessalonians 2:18 and 3:3-5 and compare what you read in 2 Thessalonians 3:1-3 with these verses.

Who is behind the evil in men? Look up Ephesians 2:1-3 and John 8:44 and record your answer in your notebook.

DAY *F*IVE

Before you complete the next assignment, consider the following verb tenses used in chapter 3. These insights will provide a greater depth of understanding into the "repeated" activities being described in 2 Thessalonians 3:6-15. Remember that the present tense in the Greek denotes continuous or habitual action. The following verbs are in the present tense. Read each verse in the light of the verb tense.

verse 6: *keep away* [33] (avoid), *leads*[34]
verse 7: *follow*
verse 8: *kept working*[35]
verse 11: *are leading,*[36] *acting like busybodies*[37]
verse 12: *work*[38]
verse 14: *do not associate*[39]
verse 15: *admonish*[40]

In 2 Thessalonians 3:4,6,12, *we command* is a repeated phrase. Look up these verses and note to whom these commands are directed and what Paul is "commanding" them to do. Compare these commands with 1 Thessalonians 4:9-12 and watch for the phrase *we commanded*.[41] What do you learn from Paul's commands? Record what you have learned in your notebook.

DAY SIX

Paul uses the words *tradition(s)*[42] two times in this second epistle. The first mention is in 2:15, and the second is in 3:6. The English transliteration of the Greek word translated *tradition* is *paradosis* and means "to deliver in teaching." It is a tradition, doctrine, or injunction delivered or communicated from one person to another. Thus, Paul writes "hold to the traditions which you were taught, whether by word *of mouth* or by letter from us" (2 Thessalonians 2:15).

Remember that there was no "New Testament" per se in Paul's day. Rather, he and others were in the process of writing it under the divine inspiration of the Holy Spirit. Thus, what Paul wrote in his epistles came to be the Word of the Lord to the church.

What was Paul's specific instruction regarding those who would not work? Record the verse in which you find this instruction in your notebook. Then list every instruction Paul gives in regard to those who lead undisciplined lives. As you make this list, note who the Thessalonians' role model is regarding a disciplined life.

Be sure that you do not overlook what the Thessalonians are to do in respect to those who do not obey Paul's instructions through this letter. Once your assignments are complete, think about what you have learned. Think about how this will help you when people who are Christians want a "free handout."

Now, having examined the word *tradition(s),* do you think we are to keep *all* traditions? Are we to give all traditions equal value with the Word of God? There are some who might say, "Yes." However, this is not what Jesus said. Look up Mark 7:1-13 and mark every occurrence of *tradition(s).* As you look at this word, notice how the context helps you understand how this usage of *tradition* differs from its usage in 2 Thessalonians.

Remember, Beloved, that we now have the completed Word of God. According to 2 Timothy 3:16,17, God's Word is all you need for every good work of life. It is your plumb line. If any tradition of man is not found in the Word of God or supported by it, then it is just that—a tradition of man. What a contrast this is with the use of tradition in 2 Thessalonians where the context uses it to refer to the solid God-inspired doctrine Paul is teaching.

Fill in your last chapter theme for 2 Thessalonians and note any "LFL's" for your life.

✌🏴

DAY SEVEN

 Store in your heart: 2 Thessalonians 3:1,7, or 16.
Read and discuss: 2 Thessalonians 3.

QUESTIONS FOR DISCUSSION OR INDIVIDUAL STUDY

∼ The final chapter of Paul's epistle begins with a request for prayer.

   a. What does Paul ask the Thessalonians to pray for them (Paul, Silvanus, and Timothy)?

b. Why do you think he asks them to pray for this?

c. What did you see as you compared 1 Thessalonians 2:18 and 3:3-5 with 2 Thessalonians 3:1-3?

d. What did you learn from studying Ephesians 2:1-3 and John 8:44?

e. What did you learn about prayer simply from looking up the references made to prayer in 1 and 2 Thessalonians?

• 1 Thessalonians 1:2-5

• 1 Thessalonians 3:9-13

• 1 Thessalonians 5:17,18,25

• 2 Thessalonians 1:11,12

• 2 Thessalonians 3:1,2

∾ How can you apply what you learned to your own life?

∾ What did Paul, Silvanus, and Timothy expect from the Thessalonians in respect to the following:

a. their commands?

b. their traditions?

∾ What was meant by traditions? Discuss what you learned from 2 Thessalonians and then what you learned from Mark 7:1-13.

∾ How is the church to deal with and respond to the following:

a. those who lead undisciplined, unruly lives?

b. those who want to eat, but refuse to work?

∾ What is Paul's course of action in respect to those who will not obey his instructions?

∾ What was the model, the example, provided by Paul, Silvanus, and Timothy?

∾ What is the most significant truth or example you encountered for your own life over the last nine weeks? Why?

∾ Can you say along with the Thessalonians that you have repented and turned to Jesus Christ and are serving Him? Can you say that you are waiting for God's Son from heaven, the One God raised from the dead, the One who delivers you from the wrath to come? Are you going to stand firm?

∾ Review the content of this epistle as you share what you recorded on your AT A GLANCE chart.

∾ What is your prayer for yourself? For others?

If you are in a class setting, have the class spend time in prayer for one another.

∾ What study are you going to do next? You can't stop… you must be rooted and grounded in the whole counsel of the Word of God, Beloved, for the day of the Lord is coming and the mystery of lawlessness is already at work. You must be prepared to proclaim His Word in season and out of season because the time has arrived when many do not want sound teaching but want only teachers who will tickle their ears. Be prepared, Beloved.

THOUGHT FOR THE WEEK

"But we should always give thanks to God for you, brethren beloved by the Lord, because God has chosen you from the beginning for salvation through sanctification by the Spirit and faith in the truth. And it was for this He called you through our gospel, that you may gain the glory of our Lord Jesus Christ" (2 Thessalonians 2:13,14).

This is the way I feel about you. Although I may not know many of you personally, which is my loss, the very thought of *you* diligently studying God's Word book-by-book through The New Inductive Study Series causes me to give thanks to God for you, my friend. Just the fact that you are continuing in His Word shows you to be a true disciple of the Lord Jesus Christ or if not yet a believer, then an earnest seeker.

If you persevere in what you are learning and professing, then, as we saw when we studied 1 Thessalonians 3, it demonstrates the reality of your faith. I feel like Paul when he wrote, "Now we *really* live, if you stand firm in the Lord" (1 Thessalonians 3:8).

As you can see from these verses, God chose you from the beginning for salvation. It is a salvation which comes about through the sanctification of the Spirit AND faith in the truth. Just think, Beloved, how your faith is being built up as a result of saturating yourself with truth these past nine weeks.

And what awaits you? The glory of the Lord Jesus Christ which you will gain at His coming. "So then, brethren, stand firm and hold to the traditions which you were taught, whether by word *of mouth* or by letter from us" (2 Thessalonians 2:15).

The "letters" were what you just studied…the Word of God given through a man who stood firm. Keep the tradition, Beloved!

> *Now may the Lord of peace Himself continually grant you peace in every circumstance. The Lord be with you all! (2 Thessalonians 3:16)*

WHAT 1 & 2 THESSALONIANS TEACH ABOUT THE DAY OF THE LORD

THE PERSONAGES OF 2 THESSALONIANS 2

The Thessalonians	The Man of Lawlessness

THE PERSONAGES OF 2 THESSALONIANS 2

The Lord Jesus Christ	He Who Restrains	Those Who Perish

2 THESSALONIANS AT A GLANCE

Theme of 2 Thessalonians:

	SEGMENT DIVISIONS	CHAPTER THEMES
Author:		
Historical Setting:		1
Purpose:		
Key Words:		
		2
		3

Notes

1. NIV: *persecution*
2. NIV: *trials*
3. NIV: also *persecution, persecuted, trials*
4. NIV: *insulted*
   KJV: *shamefully entreated*
   NKJV: *spitefully treated*
5. NIV: *persecuted* or *persecution*
   KJV; NKJV: also *tribulation*
6. KJV: *Holy Ghost*
7. NIV: *trials, be persecuted, persecution*
   KJV; NKJV: also *tribulation*
8. KJV: also *charity*
9. NIV: also *till, after that*
10. KJV: *Holy Ghost*
11. NIV; KJV; NKJV: *trouble(d)*
12. NIV: *trials*
    KJV; NKJV: *tribulation(s)*
13. KJV; NKJV: *suffer*
14. NIV: also *majesty, honored*
15. NIV: *brothers*
16. KJV; NKJV: *therefore*
17. KJV; NKJV: *man of sin*
18. KJV; NKJV: *therefore*

19. NIV: *at that time*
    KJV: *say*

20. NIV: *great distress*
    KJV; NKJV: *great tribulation*

21. NIV: *immediately after the distress of those days*

22. NIV: *at that time*

23. NIV: *the one who now holds it back*
    KJV: *he who now letteth*

24. NIV: *those who are perishing*
    KJV: *them that perish*

25. KJV; NKJV: *the day of Christ*

26. NIV: *will not come until*
    KJV: *shall not come, except*

27. NKJV: *therefore*

28. NIV: *saying that the day of the Lord has already come*
    KJV: *as that the day of Christ is at hand*
    NKJV: *as though the day of Christ had come*

29. NIV: *has already come*
    KJV: *is at hand*
    NKJV: *had come*

30. KJV; NKJV: The word *model* is not used in this chapter.

31. KJV: *ensample*

32. NIV: *not idle, idle*
    KJV; NKJV: *disorderly*

33. NASB (1977): *keep aloof*
    KJV; NKJV: *withdraw*

34. NIV: *is*
    KJV: *walketh*
    NKJV: *walks*

35. NIV; NKJV: *worked*
    KJV: *wrought*

36. NIV: *are idle*
    KJV: *which walk*
    NKJV: *who walk*

37. NIV; KJV; NKJV: *are busybodies*

38. NIV: *earn*

39. KJV: *have no company*
    NKJV: *do not keep company*

40. NIV: *warn*

41. NIV: *we told*
    KJV: *command*

42. NIV: *teaching(s)*

NOTES FOR PERSONAL STUDY

Notes for Personal Study

Notes for Personal Study

NOTES FOR PERSONAL STUDY

NOTES FOR PERSONAL STUDY

Books in the New Inductive Study Series

❧❧❧❧

Teach Me Your Ways
Genesis, Exodus,
Leviticus, Numbers,
Deuteronomy

*Choosing Victory,
Overcoming Defeat*
Joshua, Judges, Ruth

Desiring God's Own Heart
1 & 2 Samuel,
1 Chronicles

Come Walk in My Ways
1 & 2 Kings, 2 Chronicles

*Overcoming Fear and
Discouragement*
Ezra, Nehemiah, Esther

*God's Blueprint for
Bible Prophecy*
Daniel

The Call to Follow Jesus
Luke

*The Holy Spirit
Unleashed in You*
Acts

*God's Answers for
Relationships and Passions*
1 & 2 Corinthians

*Free from Bondage
God's Way*
Galatians, Ephesians

That I May Know Him
Philippians, Colossians

*Standing Firm in
These Last Days*
1 & 2 Thessalonians

*Walking in Power, Love,
and Discipline*
1 & 2 Timothy, Titus

*Living with Discernment
in the End Times*
1 & 2 Peter, Jude

Behold, Jesus Is Coming!
Revelation

HARVEST HOUSE BOOKS
BY KAY ARTHUR

༄ ༄ ༄ ༄

Beloved
God, Are You There?
How to Study Your Bible
Israel, My Beloved (A Novel)
Lord, Teach Me to Pray in 28 Days
A Marriage Without Regrets
A Marriage Without Regrets Audiobook
A Marriage Without Regrets Study Guide
A Moment with God
My Savior, My Friend
Speak to My Heart, God
With an Everlasting Love (A Novel)

Discover 4 Yourself
Inductive Bible Studies for Kids

How to Study Your Bible for Kids
God's Amazing Creation (Genesis 1–2)
Digging Up the Past (Genesis 3–11)
Joseph—God's Superhero (Genesis 37–50)
Wrong Way, Jonah! (Jonah)
Jesus in the Spotlight (John 1–11)
Jesus—Awesome Power, Awesome Love (John 11–16)
Jesus—To Eternity and Beyond! (John 17–21)
Boy, Have I Got Problems! (James)
Lord, Teach Me to Pray for Kids

Everybody, Everywhere, Anytime, Anyplace, Any Age...
Can Discover the Truth for Themselves

In today's world with its often confusing and mixed messages, where can you turn to find the answer to the challenges you and your family face? Whose word can you trust? Where can you turn when you need answers—about relationships, your children, your future?

The <u>Updated</u> *New Inductive Study Bible*

Open *this* study Bible and you will soon discover its uniqueness— unlike any other, this study Bible offers no notes, commentaries, or the opinions of others telling you what the Scripture is saying. It is in fact the only study Bible based entirely on the *inductive* study approach, providing you with instructions and the tools for observing what the text really says, interpreting what it means, and applying its principles to your life.

The only study Bible containing the *inductive study method* taught and endorsed by Kay Arthur and Precept Ministries.

• A new *smaller* size makes it easier to carry • individualized instructions for studying *every* book • guides for color marking keywords and themes • *Updated* NASB text • *improved* in-text maps and charts • 24 pages of full-color charts, historical timelines, & maps • self-discovery in its truest form

One Message, The Bible.
One Method, Inductive.

A SIMPLE, PROVEN APPROACH TO LETTING GOD'S WORD CHANGE YOUR LIFE...FOREVER

HARVEST HOUSE™
P U B L I S H E R S
EUGENE, OREGON

DIGGING DEEPER

❧❧❧❧

Books in the New Inductive Study Series are survey courses. If you want to do a more in-depth study of a particular book of the Bible, we suggest that you do a Precept Upon Precept Bible Study Course on that book. The Precept studies require approximately five hours of personal study a week. You may obtain more information on these powerful courses by contacting Precept Ministries International at 800-763-8280, visiting our website at www.precept.org, or filling out and mailing the response card in the back of this book.

If you desire to expand and sharpen your skills, you would really benefit by attending a Precept Ministries Institute of Training. The Institutes are conducted throughout the United States, Canada, and in a number of other countries. Class lengths vary from one to five days, depending on the course you are interested in. For more information on the Precept Ministries Institute of Training, call Precept Ministries.